George D. Herron

A Plea for the Gospel

George D. Herron

A Plea for the Gospel

ISBN/EAN: 9783337888350

Printed in Europe, USA, Canada, Australia, Japan

Cover: Foto ©Lupo / pixelio.de

More available books at **www.hansebooks.com**

A PLEA FOR THE GOSPEL.

BY

GEORGE D. HERRON,

NEW YORK: 46 East Fourteenth St.
THOMAS Y. CROWELL & CO.
BOSTON: 100 Purchase Street.

I DEDICATE THIS PLEA FOR THE GOSPEL TO
MY WIFE,

Mary Eberhard Herron,

WHO HAS BEEN TO ME A LIVING CONSCIENCE.

PREFACE.

THESE four sermons were prepared to preach to preachers. "The Peril of the Church" and "The Opportunity of the Church" were delivered before clerical unions in western cities. "The Reality of Faith" and "The Faith that Overcometh the World" were preached before state ecclesiastical associations. Fragments of these sermons have been widely published and discussed, and many calls have been made for their publication in this permanent form. This call has been emphasized by the interest awakened by the publication of four sermons, a year ago, under the title of "The Larger Christ."

The burden of that book is the burden of this. The revelation of the sovereign love of Christ as the law of all human life is the thought which lies at the heart of each discourse, accounting for whatever repetition of expression, or exaggeration of emphasis, the critic may find. The assertion of the cross as the eternal principle of all divine and human action, not simply the accident of sin, seems to me the imperative of the hour. This one thing I do. I can find no other work. Everything I touch resolves itself into the message of the cross. So I accept this message as my intellectual and moral portion, rejoicing in the larger and more comprehensive word which other voices will speak.

These sermons are not put forth as dogma, but as life, fragmentary, indeed, but yet life. May the living Christ bless them as food to some hungry souls in this day of human need and divine opportunity!

G. D. H.

First Congregational Church.
  BURLINGTON, Io., June, 1892.

CONTENTS.

I.
Unconsecrated Service the Peril of the Church . . . 1

II.
The Opportunity of the Church 33

III.
The Reality of Faith 57

IV.
The Faith that overcometh the World . . . 85

I.

UNCONSECRATED SERVICE THE PERIL OF THE CHURCH.

THE essential of Philistinism is self-satisfaction, — the belief that one has the best there is, and that he has all he needs. This is a faith held by many excellent people, who are, nevertheless, enemies of the light, of progress, and, in a way, of truth, who, above all, fail to achieve the highest and noblest aims. For the mood of progress is the mood of discontent, of feeling that one is not what he ought to be, that one has not the best to be had, and that of the excellent things which he does possess he does not possess enough. The satisfied man is always an inferior man. The superior man is always dissatisfied; his goals and his achievements are before him. No matter what they may have been in the past, nor how greatly the world may have honored them, his real life always lies in advance. The passion for perfection is the sign of the noblest kind of character and mind, and it is this passion which breeds what has been called " divine discontent." It is not restlessness nor rebellion, but the feeling that one must always be doing and being better. This is the feeling of the great artists; no achievement satisfies. There is always the intense desire to do something still better; and it is this desire and the steady realization of it, rather than any recognition or reward, which gives life its zest and its interest. — *Hamilton W. Mabie.*

We have too much barbarian blood in our veins, and we lack measure, harmony, and grace. Christianity, in breaking man up into outer and inner, the world into earth and heaven, hell and paradise, has decomposed the human unity, in order, it is true, to reconstruct it more profoundly and more truly. But Christianity has not yet digested this powerful leaven. She has not yet conquered the true humanity; she is still living under the antinomy of sin and grace, of here below and there above. She has not penetrated into the whole heart of Jesus. She is still in the narthex of penitence; she is not reconciled, and even the churches still wear the livery of service, and have none of the joy of the daughters of God baptized of the Holy Spirit. — *Amiel's Journal.*

A PLEA FOR THE GOSPEL.

I.

UNCONSECRATED SERVICE THE PERIL OF THE CHURCH.

And it came to pass on the way at the lodging place, that the Lord met him, and sought to kill him. — Ex. iv. 24.

It is a strange incident in the life of Moses that is thus briefly and obscurely stated. From the beginning of his career Moses had been driven about with the sense of a divine compulsion, his life taken from his own disposal, his ways and times other than his own choosing. Early called to be the deliverer of the Hebrew people from their Egyptian bondage, he had been driven from his task, into an exile of forty years, at his first attempt to fulfil his mission. After the long waiting, — doubtless through alternating periods of hope and despair, — God saw that the man was sufficiently humbled by failure and purified by suffering to begin his work. By the time the cup of Israel's affliction was full, the years of divine discipline had added to the natural strength of Moses' character something of the wisdom and the patience of the power of God. So, while one day tending the flocks of his Midianite father-in-law, God spoke to him from the burning bush, bidding him go down into Egypt and lead forth the chosen people to their promised land. After some halting and arguing with God, Moses took his family and started for Egypt, according to the divine command. Yet, on the way, while hastening along the path in which God himself had set the leader's feet, God met him and sought to kill him. This is the simple and inspired way of saying that something happened to Moses, something came into or upon his life, that threatened to destroy it, and defeat his divinely directed plans for delivering Israel. And what else could this arrested journey, this mortal struggle for life and faith and wisdom, — what else could it be than the overpowering and consecrating presence of the Lord? Hold on, Moses; wait a little; think awhile; understand yourself; look at me. Either you must make a complete and trustful surrender of yourself to me, so that I may work in you, and you may work with me, unhindered by any self-will or unbelief, or you must get out of my way. It is better you should die than that you should take up my work with unconsecrated hands. To this end have I brought this upon you, for this reason have I permitted this thing to come into your life, that I may render you self-helpless, leaving you no choice but death or irrevocable self-surrender. Choose now, Moses, with a choice that shall be eternal.

It may be the Lord appeared to Moses just as he appears to all of us, in those great epochal moments when we lie very low under his humbling hand, terribly conscious that nowhere in the universe is there sustaining strength save in the healing touch of his infinite life; nowhere any hope save in the reviving breath of his infinite mercy. If we would receive him, the Lord would meet us in every disappointment and affliction, calling us to a sincerer self-examination, helping us to a purer and completer consecration; he would make every sorrow the sanctuary in which we should enter into a closer fellowship with his life. It is true, we ought to see opportunities for a deeper and more unbroken intimacy with God in our joys, as well as perils and griefs; but we see the heavens best in the night.

It costs God much to make a man; it costs a man to have God make him. Out of the lowest depths of self-abasement God lifts men to the greatest heights. Every man called to do a great work has been baffled in his efforts until the reins of his purposes were delivered into the hand mightier than his own; or he has been kept humble by relentless memories of sin, and baptized with sorrows that would consume his life if he abode not in the secret place of the Most High; or he has been led under the despotism of passions that would become demoniac if not hallowed upon the altar of a perfect sacrifice. From the poverty and bondage of a self-life, into the unsearchable riches and infinite freedom of the divine life, there is a vast wilderness of experience, tracked only by paths of fearless faith; and few there be that find them. Those who find their way from the old life into the new have left behind them wasted years, and the wrecks of wicked hopes that once seemed divine. It seems as though human self-will compels God to lose immense quantities of the strongest and purest lives, in order to save some precious fragments to invest with an altogether divine quality. Again and again, at the point of death, are the messengers of God delivered from the peril of unconsecrated service ere they are allowed to proceed upon their redemptive errands.

Yet God counts no price too great to pay for a man. The human character that is eternal has been wrought out by the suffering of God. By the sorrow of his heart has God chiselled out his image in the soul of man. By the blood of the Lamb slain from the foundation of the world are we cleansed from the sins of time. But God reckons not the cost; he spared not his Son; he quenches not his sufferings. And without stint God lavishes suffering upon every son, who thereby learns obedience. It is worth God's while. There is no sight so sublime, no beauty so enthralling, no influence so subtle in operation and measureless in results, no power so resistless, as that of a human life wholly consecrated to God. The most splendid and authoritative institutions of men are toys compared to the pure-hearted child of God who has seen the divine meanings of things, and yielded all his powers to the absolute sway of the eternal realities. He who is great enough to put the kingdoms of the world and all their glory behind him, rather than forfeit one tittle of his birthright as a son of God ; who falters not in the face of the darkest mysteries of life, and drinks deep of its sorrows that he may have fellowship with God ; who dares be led from day to day by his divine instincts, without anxiety for the morrow ; whose communion with God is so close and unbroken that prayer is his soul's atmosphere ; whose religious knowledge is not the traditions of men, but the word of God in his inmost being ; who speaks what he hears God speak, and does the works he sees God doing;— such a man, soever humble though he be, is the real maker of civilizations, the divine reformer of nations, the eternal worker of righteousness. God has provided and man has discovered no greater force to work out the redemption of the race than that of the wholly unselfish life that seeketh not its own. It is not with institutions and formulas, so much as with men, that God unfolds his own life in the development of humanity — men in whom he can have his loving and righteous way; men with a faith as insuppressible as light; men who are incarnations of his drawing sacrificial love.

To those who value what they can see and own more than what is unseen and eternal this does not always seem to be true. Such as regard the social respectabilities above Christliness of life may delight to honor the selfish man who accepts the church's creeds and observes the commercial moralities. The church may invite to high places men of renowned integrity and conspicuous philanthropy, who long since have exchanged the hand of brotherhood with which God created them for the polished hand and steely grasp of covetousness. Yet all service not rendered in the divine and living Christ-way is but the service of death. It is the unconsecrated service which is the peril and infidelity of the church.

The church may appear to be growing in aggressiveness and influence in other than the meek and lowly ways of Christ, without being rejected by the proud, and acquainted with the grief of the stricken and oppressed; without being smitten with the sorrows, and wounded with the transgressions of the straying sheep; without pouring out its soul unto death in manifesting the saving love of God for a lost world. But when the church is holding conventions and congratulating itself on its progress, it may be changing into a sepulchre of death, full of the bones of religious bigotry and the corruption of social pride. It may be conquering the world in its fancy, while in reality it is being conquered by the world. It may have become so servile in its deference to the customs of a pagan society and an atheistic market, so blind and bitter in its defence of dead forms of religious truth, as to be as incapable of seeing its actual condition as death is incapable of seeing life. The world may have flattered and bribed it into the surrender of the power to discern its own spiritual degradation, its moral emaciation, its sad departure from the spirit and life of its Lord.

The Jewish church had reached this state when the Son of God appealed to it for the recognition of his messianic authority. There were saintly men and women in the temple and synagogues, praying for the redemption, and waiting for the consolation, of Israel. The temple and its services had been the object of God's particular care through long and weary centuries. Often had God visited and corrected his people Israel. They were the treasurers of the oracles of God. But God cares for the sacredest institutions no more than they are his instruments for making men. When they begin to exist for themselves more than for their mission, then God destroys them. The Son of man found the Jewish church so hopelessly fixed in its own rather than God's way of salvation, that its destruction was essential to the redemption of the world. Instead of being, as its rulers thought, indispensable to the kingdom of God, it confronted the kingdom's coming with unyielding resistance. The Pharisees and scribes, many of them men of profound religious culture and eminent piety, were the only utterly abhorrent and apparently incurable souls that Jesus met in his ministry. It was a case of consecration or death that confronted the Jews; and they chose death, not knowing the day of their visitation, wilfully blind to their eternal opportunity. The peril of unconsecrated service plunged Christendom into the blood and anguish of the Reformation, when the eyes of Savonarola and Wickliffe, Luther and Zwingli, were open to see, and their mouths open to hail, the coming of Christ in a diviner order of history. On the pages of Catholic records were lustrous deeds, and the names of devoted martyrs who loved not their lives unto death. Before the heroic purity and passionate consecration of Bernard of Clairvaux and Francis of Assissi, and the self-sacrifice of a great multitude whom no man can number, we may well be dumb at the wonder of their lives and the shame of our own poor zeal and faith; when we can match their loyalty to Christ, then we may have a right to point out their superstition and folly. But the church, withal, was in God's way. As an institution it had come to exist for its own sake, making religion the disgust of intelligence, the suspicion of moral honesty, and the protection of blackest crimes. It had juggled with righteousness, and distorted the truth, until the world was well-nigh ceasing to believe in the reality of righteousness or the existence of truth. Better the church should have been swept from the face of the earth than have remained consecrated to selfish ends! Those who came out from the church were its saviours. The birth of Protestantism was the salvation of Catholicism. Only by some measure of consecration, somewhere within itself, could the church universal escape dissolution. Unconsecrated service always carries in it the germs of the servant's death.

But the Reformation did not restore the gospel. It did not liberate it from the tyranny of Roman legalism, or clear it of the fungus of Greek philosophy. Few pulpits have any intelligent conception of what Christianity really is; that which the mass of Protestant preachers proclaim is not the gospel. Christ came into the world not so much to found a religion, as to reveal the religion hidden beneath all the *débris* of discarded beliefs and abandoned forms of worship. He taught that religion was pure and simple life; life with God, life free from all fear of nature or distrust of God, life rich with the fulness of human fellowships. It was life as sweet and joyous and unaffected in its relation to God, as that of the little child to the loving parent; a life of whole-hearted surrender to Christ's way of living, Christ's way of thinking, Christ's way of working; a life of personal and direct contact with God in Christ, without the intervention of rituals, priests, or creeds; a life that could joyously endure the loss of all worldly favors and material possessions for the sake of realizing its divine childhood, and bringing others into the knowledge and glory of that childhood. To give men this sonship, Christ came, himself the resurrection of the divine life in man — which is religion — from the ruins of ages of distrust, idolatry, and disobedience. He rescued this divine life of fellowship with God and brotherhood with man from the dominion of selfishness, wounded and bleeding, corrupt and deformed, as the life was, and healed it with the balm of infinite mercy, and gave it back to man. The gospel was God's good news that the divinely human life could be lived; that whereas in times past ceremonies and systems had been necessary because of the blindness of human unbelief and the darkness of human understanding, the time was now come when men, through Christ, could have immediate access unto the Father. Christ, in his loving life and sacrificial death, revealed the forgiveness and mercy, the gracious power of the Father's love. After the cross, men could have no excuse for doubting the love of God; after the ascension of Christ and his return in the Spirit there was no excuse for abiding in unrighteousness. God was no Jupiter or Cæsar. He made no exactions concerning the past. His love needed no bribing. His vengeance was satisfied with man's repentance. It was the prodigal who had gone away from the Father, not the Father away from the prodigal. The blood of Calvary was the witness and pledge of God's unchanging friendship for man. Then Christ revealed to men how they might be the children of their Father, sons of God, by being like him. This is the meaning of the Sermon on the Mount. God is good; God is forgiving unto the uttermost; God loves those who hate him, blesses those who curse, bestows his favors on the false and unjust, suffers in behalf of those whose sins are an abomination in his eyes. Therefore, be like God and you will be his children. Follow me; live as I live; be as I am; trust your lives to my leadership; do the works you see me do; eat my bread, drink my drink; make my righteousness yours; be natural like the lily, like the little child; be spiritual, living as I live, in the light of an immediate vision of God. This way of living is not hard; this burden of love for my brothers is not grievous; this yoke of my Father's will is easy; I walk in no darkness. Follow me; then you will walk in the light in which I walk; you will have the cross to bear I bear, and my mission of redemption through sacrifice will be yours; but you will have the peace that makes me strong, the joy that overflows my life, and the love for men by which I glorify my Father in their eyes.

This was the gospel. This was the faith that was delivered to the apostles. It was the good news of forgiveness; the joyful tidings that the world was redeemed; the gift of a power to work righteousness; the revelation of God as the Father of man, and of man as the child of the Father. Every vestige of a veil between man and God was torn away; no conditions, no opinions, were put between them, save repentance and faith. They were not asked to believe anything about God except that he was good and forgiving, and would give them his own power to be good and forgiving, if they would repent of their sins, and take up the Christ-life of obedient faith. In the joy of this simple gospel of redemption the apostles went forth, empowered with triumphant righteousness, on jubilant feet of peace, to conquer the world for God. The like of their glorious faith and mighty works had never been seen before, and has rarely been seen since. Christ had overcome the world. It was not the devil's world, but God's world.

Soon Christianity came in contact with Greek philosophy. The gospel was too simple for the Greeks; they would adopt it on a philosophic basis. I do not believe, with Dr. Edwin Hatch, that the Sermon on the Mount is the centre of Christianity, or that conduct is its basis. Christianity is a life, a divine incarnation. Christianity is the life of God in man, revealed in the incarnation of Jesus Christ, the cross its basic principle. But I do believe, with Dr. Hatch, that the Greeks changed Christianity from a message of righteousness into a theology. They shifted the seat of religious judgment from character to opinion, exalting dogma above life. They grafted into the gospel a philosophic Trinity of which the apostles had never heard. Then Christianity grappled with civil Romanism, and the empire was finally converted into a great ecclesiastical structure, and Christianity became a despotic government, instead of simple life with God. God's fatherhood became a Cæsarhood. Christ the Redeemer and elder brother of men became a successful pleader at the bar of an infinite judge, in a court of abstract and unreal justice; a judge who had nothing to do with the reality of love. Instead of being received as a revelation of God, Christ has since been presented as a protection from God.

Divine and great, beyond all reckoning, was the work of the reformers. But there remains a greater work to be done. There has been a reformation: the work that remains is a restoration of Christianity; an emancipation of the gospel from baneful bondage to the Greeks, who have fettered its freedom and bruised its life through all the centuries of its progress; a deliverance of Christianity from the Romans, who have corrupted our very language with their unvital legalism of thought; whose law, Hegel says, makes a definition of humanity impossible.

The time has come when the church must be started upon a new career — a career that will give back Christianity to Christendom, and restore the faith of the apostles to a waiting and expectant world. From the prison-house of churchly selfishness, from the bonds of dogmatic theology, the gospel must be set free, or there will arise a new Protestantism. In the problems of our day Christ comes to call the church to a more comprehensive mission. Except the church be born again, and a heart of flesh take the place of its heart of pride, it cannot see the kingdom of God, which is pressing in upon it from the future. To this work God now calls the church to consecrate, yea, perhaps to sacrifice, its freshest thought, its most passionate devotion, its bravest hearts, its strongest lives, that the unsearchable riches of Christ may be poured afresh upon an impoverished world, and all men be made to see what is the dispensation of the mystery which from all ages hath been hid in God, waiting for the manifestation of his Son and the preparation of the earth for a regenerated society, a heavenly civilization. To this end must these be dedicated, or the church will perish like the temple, or be rent like Rome. The Spirit calls upon the church to furnish prophetic souls who will feel the anger of the infinite love against the covetousness which has betrayed Christ to be crucified at the hands of mammon. There is a divine inconsistency that drives the prophets of larger truth beyond the realm of logic and opinion into the sphere of infinite liberty, where the Spirit utters through them the thoughts of God:— these the church needs, for these the churchless multitudes wait, to lead them through the trial hour that is coming upon the whole earth. The church must raise up men who will obey the Spirit's voice, or it must get out of God's way. For what cares God for churches, if they obstruct the march of the divine purposes?

Do not think I would detract any honor from

the innumerable company of saints and martyrs, scholars and missionaries, who by their heroic lives of service have gathered the glory of God about our Protestant Christianity, and have made the race rich with their sacrifices. These cannot be too highly honored. But we truly honor the brave and good who have been faithful in the great crises of the past, and broken the old bonds, and pioneered the race's way into larger futures, by being ourselves true and fearless in welcoming the new life and meeting the fateful crises of our day of opportunity. We never dishonor the truth and faith of the past so much as when we try to make them the defence of our own stupidity and cowardice.

We know, when we consider the matter intelligently and honestly, that Christianity is not fulfilling its mission of establishing the righteousness of God, as it is defined in the Sermon on the Mount and revealed in the incarnation and by the cross, as the basis of human society. The world is conquering the church, at this moment, as truly as the church is conquering the world. The church itself would regard the attempt to realize the prophetic and apostolic vision of a new earth as not only hopeless lunacy, but a dangerous and disreputable movement towards the disruption of society. There is nothing which the vested interests of conservative Protestantism resent so much as the kingdom of God, which is the brotherhood of man. The world knows the church is failing; that it has become a secular more than a Christian institution. The divine common-sense of man discerns a difference between the Christianity of Christ and the Christianity of the modern church which cannot be reconciled. The world of doubt believes that the gospel, if emancipated from philosophy and actually practised, would cure all the ills and solve all the problems of society. There is more vital faith in much of the scepticism and heresy of our day than in a great deal of what we call orthodoxy. There is more hunger for righteousness in the unrest that is slowly gathering into mighty storms on the horizon of human hope than in the self-satisfaction and religious complacency of the church. The children of darkness are seeing the signs of the times more clearly than the children of light. Again is God hiding his mighty purposes from the wise and prudent, and revealing them unto babes. We need to ask ourselves earnestly whether the Son of man, if he should suddenly come into our churches, would find among us the faith that overcometh the world.

We point to our costly and beautiful temples of worship, to the crosses crowning the village hill-tops, and the crosses the church spires lift above the city's smoke and strife. We count our great missionary benefactions, and hold mammoth religious conventions. We are perfecting and unifying our great ecclesiastical organizations, and forming new societies, and appointing countless committees. We have revised creeds, and progressive theologies, and renowned preachers. But all the while the church is getting farther and farther away from the lost sheep it was sent to save. The covetousness that fattens on the flesh of toiling boys and girls; the greed that wrecks the hopes and fortunes of less cunning rivals; the fashion whose fatuous arrogance fans the flame of judgment that is kindling in the skies; the luxury that is content to enjoy, while men with dark thoughts beg for work, and hopeless women slave in sweaters' dens, and the life withers out of starved babes; — all these smile and bow and pray in the church, while the great sad, suspicious world impatiently waits to see whether God be living or dead. This is not Christianity. This is not according to the gospel of Jesus Christ. Much of what we call Christianity is no less than an aristocratic and shameless pauperism, thriving on the wealth of sacrifice inherited from the past; resting in high-priced pews and fashionable residences; cunningly squeezing a luxurious living out of humanity, and superciliously labelling as charity the appeals made to serve the humanity that supports it. It is the victorious forces of time the church worships — prudence, thrift, respectability, reputation, culture — while it is practically infidel to the Christian gospel. We hear wise men, indeed, "preaching up truth and preaching down error" from the pulpit; but it is nearly always theological error, while a refined brutality practises, under the church's protection, a conscienceless and defiant atheism. Religious papers deplore the influence of money in politics, but seem innocent of the fact that money has no less influence, if not more, in securing certains kinds of ecclesiastical prominence, in obtaining positions of trust in religious corporations, than in securing seats in our national legislature. Our social system, even where it is churchly, is not Christian, but respectable paganism, galvanized with Christianity. The church does not dream of practising the gospel; rather, it has practically abandoned the gospel as the law of life, putting opinion and money in its place, rearing the throne of mammon in the place of the changeless cross of the slain Christ, taking to itself the attitude of the scribes and Pharisees, instead of following the Son of God with the divine sorrow which alone can cleanse the race of sin. Unconsecrated men, who lie and rob and destroy, who outrage all humanities and gorge themselves with blood-red gold, may yet pass for men of integrity and conspicuous Christian philanthropy, whose self-satisfaction it seems cruel and unjust to disturb with the social impoliteness of the Sermon on the Mount. The church as an institution is saying, " Lord, Lord; " but its leaders are not doing, nor have they any faith in the practicability of doing, the things the Lord tells them. And I sadly fear it to be true, — would God that I might be wrong! — that the most unmoving obstacle which the coming Christ confronts in the redemption of human society, is the raw unbelief in righteousness, the nice and delicate yet no less blind and hateful infidelity to the gospel, which permeates our conservative Christianity, making the church the antagonist of the righteousness of Christ. For that church which worships Christ, and yet rejects his way of living, is the Judas Iscariot of modén Christendom.

The church must have a new career. There must be a resurrection of the gospel. An emancipated gospel is the hope of human society. For this the world prays and waits. To deliver the gospel from the weight of heathen theology, which has well-nigh smothered its life; to wrest Christianity from the distorting grasp of human selfishness; to preach the gospel in its divine simplicity and regal authority; to Christianize the church which bears Christ's name, — this is the work which calls all the sons of God who are ready to make themselves of no reputation in the eyes of the Pharisees, and be despised and rejected by the self-indulgent worshippers of mammon. The self-willed infidelity, the incurable unbelief, which an apostolic faith must scourge from the church, before the Son of man can lead it forth in the victory of righteousness which shall bring in the thousand years of peace, is that faith which tries to be a substitute for life. The church which, under the cover of dogma, disbelieves in the power of Christ to lead us out of actual selfishness; which believes that men can be saved from sin by holding certain opinions about God, without ceasing from sin; which impugns the honesty of God by assuming that he never intended us to do as his eternal Son tells us; which presumes that God would promulgate a divine gospel which is unnatural law, and which man cannot practise; which puts forth Christ's righteousness as something to take the place of our own, so that we can go on enjoying the world's comforts, and gaining its profits according to its covetous customs;—not by such a church will God convert the race. God will never permit a church which does not itself believe the gospel, or pretend to obey it, to carry the gospel to every creature. Nor will the divine intelligence of humanity receive a theology that teaches a salvation from sin without ceasing from sin; for, however needful and progressive such a theology may once have been, it has done its work; and, in the increasing light of the grace that shines from the face of the healing Christ, is naught but an unholy superstition. No revision of creeds, no holding of conventions, no flaunting of banners, no missionary enthusiasm, can evade the supreme and epochal issue which now confronts the church, in this the beginning of the most revolutionary period of Christian history. The question the church must answer, the question which converges all gone and coming historic crises, carrying in itself the solution of all human problems, is this: Is the gospel practicable? does God mean it? is redemption a reality? has Christ overcome the world? is the Christ who is in us greater than the devil of selfishness without us? Until the church — I trust not at the point of death — enters upon a searching self-examination, and decides whether it really believes in this gospel, whether it accepts or rejects it, the conversion of the world to Christianity is the very vanity of our moral imbecility. If the church tries to evade this supreme moment of its history, persisting in preaching the gospel of theology instead of the living Christ; if it revels in the glory of the past, and rejoices in its heritage in the present, without presenting itself as a living and unblemished sacrifice unto God; if it continues to hide from the world, in the interests of social selfishness and dogmatic theology, what Christianity really is; if it persists in a wordy loyalty to its creeds, and infidelity to the Sermon on the Mount; then God will meet it upon the way upon which he sent it, in its palaces of vain worship, and leave not one stone of its goodly temples upon another.

I have said all this, my brothers, because I am an optimist; because I believe in the divine life in man ; because I see that the kingdom of heaven is at hand. If I were a pessimist I should glorify what is, rather than herald the better that is to be. The world is redeemed. Our Redeemer lives, and his Spirit reigns, and there is no more excuse for our abiding in unrighteousness. This is God's world, and the laws of God are more practicable than the laws of the devil. This was the faith of the apostles. It is the faith which the Spirit of God has wrung from the agony of apostolic souls since the rapt John saw the Christ of judgment moving in the progress of the ages towards their divine consumation in the new earth of righteousness, resting in the eternal Sabbath of God, communistic with the ensphering love of the new heaven.

To the work of restoring Christianity to Christendom, of giving back the gospel unto men, the coming Christ now calls us. To the measure that we put reputation and happiness, position and possessions, affections and all sacred interests, upon the altar of a perfect sacrifice, taking willingly for our portion whatever lot he assigns us, believing in the righteousness of our cause and the rectitude of our course, loving not our lives unto death, to that measure will the joy that was set before him be our joy, and his glory our throne. And he will keep us in the hour of trial that is to come quickly upon the whole world, and write upon us his own name, and the name of the new Jerusalem which cometh down out of heaven from God.

II.

THE OPPORTUNITY OF THE CHURCH.

THE disastrous results of a diffusion of Christianity at the cost of its intensity is very apparent to those of us who are greatly interested in the social problems of the present moment. . . . It is quite beyond all question that, according to the intention of Christ, the Christian church should at all times represent a body living not only by a certain rule of faith, but also by a certain moral law, which puts the sternest restraints on the spirit of competition, on the acquisition of wealth, on selfish aggrandizement; which bids every man, in the simplest sense, love his neighbor as himself; which enjoins the bearing of one another's burdens, as the only fulfilling of the law of Christ. It is difficult to imagine that a New-Testament Christian could have doubted that he had to carry his religion into all the affairs of life, or could have been in the least surprised if his religion involved his being poorer than one of his non-Christian neighbors who was not bound by the obligations of the church. How is it then that we have reached a condition of things when men cannot only utter, as multitudes of men always have done, the maxims of worldliness and selfishness, but utter these maxims without any sense that, by simply giving expression to them, they are repudiating Christianity, as far as words go, quite as really as if they were denying the Christian creed, or as if in the old days of persecution they had offered incense to the divinity of the Roman emperor? . . . — *Principal Charles Gore.*

Have we learnt it yet — this eternal message of love, this good tidings of spiritual freedom, this character of heavenly privileges, this birthright of spiritual blessing? Nay, rather have not we and our fathers so obscured it by the blinding veil of our dogmatisms, ritualisms, and sabbatisms, that a weary world is crying out to us to-day, "Restore to us the Christianity of Christ"? May God give strength and volume to the voice of that righteous, that agonized demand, until we, the teachers, pressed onward by the spirit within and the urgency without, shall trample underfoot the galling tradition of the elders and speak at length with the accents of Christ's simple love. . . . — *Bishop Moorhouse.*

THE OPPORTUNITY OF THE CHURCH.

Behold, I have set before thee a door opened, which none can shut. — REV. iii. 8.

THE more I read the Revelation of John, the more I receive it as the message of a great soul whose vision of God had been clarified by deep sufferings. The book was written while John was an exile on the isle of Patmos, during one of the early and bloody persecutions by which Rome sought, as a matter of political safety rather than of religious concern, to extinguish the Christian faith. However despicable the religion of Christ to their pride, the Romans clearly saw that the practice of its principles, if wide-spread, could not but eventually destroy the foundations of force and fraud on which imperialism rested. The whole Revelation reflects the lights and shadows of the sad and mighty days through which the church was passing, persecuted by merciless enemies without, imperilled by betrayers of the truth within. A world of heroic experiences is mirrored in the apostle's designation of himself and some of his fellow-Christians as brothers and partakers in the tribulations and patience of Jesus. He seems to have spent the time of his exile in the closest communion with God, straining the eyes of his faith to see what might be the intentions of God concerning his people. It may be that the nature of John's banishment was such that he had no refuge from pain of body and grief of mind save in making prayer his occupation. It was while communing in the heart of the Father, caught up in the eternally onward sweep of the Divine Spirit, that John found himself in company with the light-ensphered Christ of judgment, going forth in the unresting power of an all-loving righteousness to conquer all things visible and invisible by his resistless strength. With a voice like that of many waters, the Son of man bade him write all he saw and heard, giving him a distinct message for each of the seven churches which had been within the sphere of his authority. And with the reception of these messages the vision of John widened to take in the historical processes by which the kingdoms of the world were finally to be converted into the kingdom of Christ.

The message of Jesus to the church at Philadelphia was one of loving commendation and appreciative sympathy. The Philadelphian Christians were warned of the hour of trial which was about to shake and change the whole inhabited earth, and test the courage and quality of Christian believers. The new Jerusalem, by which was meant a divinely just and righteous civilization, was descending out of heaven from God; and the ransomed ages would read in the records of God that these obscure, despised, and persecuted Christians were the builders of the indestructible foundations of righteousness and truth upon which Christ was rearing, through the crisis of history, the heavenly social structure which is the theme and prophecy of the supremely mystical yet intensely practical Revelation. Thus Christ set before the faithful Philadelphians, who were trusting in the divine strength to fill up the measure of their weakness, an open door of the largest usefulness, through which they might enter the life and work of God. And none could shut it; no earthly power nor false friends; neither persecutions nor death.

The door of life swings always open, inviting every soul to larger usefulness, to a closer union with the thought and work of God. The immanent Christ is forever calling us to be better workmen of the tabernacle of love in which God is to dwell with men and make them his people. The divine voice that bids us come up higher is never silent. No human weakness can close Christ's door. No earthly power can move the hand that openeth and shutteth. No adverse circumstances can diminish the fruitfulness of human consecration. Nothing can happen to a soul, a church, or a nation, that Christ would not make an open door of consecration to greater living and diviner usefulness. The door of opportunity is always open. Unbelief may refuse to enter. But none can shut the door which Christ opens.

If man believed in the divine authority of Christ as Christ believed in the divine life in man, the redemption of the world would soon be manifested as a fact which none could deny, or would wish to deny. And the new earth of righteousness and peace would push out the old earth of injustice and strife with the speed of God's desire. Christ was the supreme idealist. He saw in all men the offspring of God. His gospel proceeds upon the assumption of the divinity of our humanity. We are made of the stuff that constitutes God. Hence our Lord knew no limit to the possibilities of human character, because he knew no limit to the gracious power of God which was working in man and causing man to work out his salvation in divine being and doing. The call of Christ is the awakening of the soul to its divine ancestry, which sin has obscured and dishonored. It is the quickening of the divine energies which sleep beneath man's moral sloth and corruption. It is a resurrection from a self-entombment into the glory of a divine childhood. It is a call to quit ourselves as men that God through us may manifest himself as God. Christ called men to reveal and realize God in the world through a divinely human sonship. He sent men to show forth, as he had done, the humanity of God in the divinity of their manhood. He uplifted men with a vision of the divine ideal of human life which was within the reach and realization of their faith. He saw men enlarging according to the greatness of their thinking. He measured character by aspiration. He appealed to man's undeveloped spiritual heroism; not to what was slavish, or fearful, or selfish, or ease-loving. The cross was in every path of spiritual growth and achievement which Christ pointed out. Every door of opportunity which he opened was a door of sacrifice.

Before the church of our day the Christ of judgment, the ruler of the kings of earth, with a countenance as the sun shining in his strength, opens wide the effectual door of the church's supreme opportunity. With a voice like the voice of many waters, gathering into itself the questions of the centuries, he is calling for a regenerated Christianity to enter and claim the earth and its fulness as God's. The Christianizing of industry, the gospelizing of commerce, the moral enforcement of the Sermon on the Mount, the proclamation of the cross as the basic principle of society, is the work that is now before the church. The opportunity of the church is the brotherhood of man. Buying and selling, work and wages, must be converted into divine sacraments of human fellowship. The fate of Christianity itself is at stake in meeting the problems of society and finance. If the church does not take up these responsibilities, and set itself about righting the wrongs that are making the few rich and the many poor, putting strife between classes, making enemies of men who should be brothers, the church will fail in the greatest opportunity the Lord Christ has put in its hands; and he will make a new church. Until the church takes hold of these problems in the spirit and power of the gospel — and that only is sufficient to solve these questions — insisting that men can and must obey the gospel, then in multiplying our churches we are making ropes of sand;

doing work that shall have to be done over again in purer and braver days. It is essential atheism, it is to worship a powerless God and believe in a dead Christ, to presume that our industrial system, with its poverty and wealth, its war and want, its inequality of distribution, can endure. The pulpit must teach that it is the business of the employer to so conduct his affairs that the fatherhood of God and brotherhood of man shall be facts in his establishment. If Christianity has any authority, and I believe it has all authority, it must produce men who will as truly trade and work for righteousness' sake as the pulpit is supposed to preach for righteousness' sake. And why does it seem to Christian men unreasonable that a human being should toil, invent, and do business, for the good of others than himself? Why cannot a man work as faithfully and wisely for benefits which his fellow-men are to enjoy as for his own selfish profit and enjoyment? Why does it seem strange to the twentieth century of Christian history that a man should be stimulated to far higher endeavors, to more untiring efforts, to build up industry for the benefit of society rather than his own selfish benefit? Why in the name of reason and righteousness, in the name of the suffering Christ, cannot a man be as fertile and energetic in doing business for righteousness' sake as in doing business for his own sake?

The answer to these questions, the remedy for social inequality, cannot be found in what we understand by modern benevolence. The gifts of money to endow colleges and replenish missionary funds from the hands of extortionate wealth are a simple evasion of the whole social problem, and a trifling with God. Instead of making the future hopeful, such philanthropy is the most hopeless feature in the social propsect. Gifts to universities and libraries and hospitals on the part of covetousness and bribery and greed are disgusting to the soul of God. The flattering of such givers as these by the church not only abominably falsifies the gospel of Christ, but makes the lost sheep of the house of Israel the suspicious enemies of the church Christ sent to be their friend. Never ought the church to feel such utter shame as when beholding its leaders scheming to get gifts of money made possible only by entire infidelity to the gospel of righteousness. The jubilees which the church holds in honor of the so-called benefactions of stock-gamblers and railroad-wreckers, of trust monopolists and oppressors of the poor, are but a ridiculous and ill-disguised religious hookwinkery. Christ did not send his church into the world to get the money of mammon, but to defend the oppressed, denounce wickedness, establish justice, and work righteousness. Christ did not receive Zaccheus, the rich publican, because he made an offering of money, but because he repented of his sins and restored fourfold his wrongly exacted gains. The church not only betrays Christ, who was the most terrible of all prophets in his condemnation of extortion and covetousness, but, in the long run, materially as well as morally loses by its shameful cowardice. If there is any truth in the gospel worth living for, or worth dying for, it is the truth that men are their brothers' keepers. If the gospel is true and authoritative, it is the most imperative duty of the church to lift up an unceasing complaint against our social and financial evils, against progress by the ruin and impoverishment of society, against the under-payment of wages, against the present interpretation of the law of supply and demand, until these shall be relegated to the museum of history, to take their place with the tomahawk and scalping-knife, the pirate ship and inquisition rack.

Christianity came into the world as a fellowship, a brotherhood. Christ came not as a theologian; nor were the apostles theologians. Christ's doctrines were not theological, but social. Christ was the revelation of a life — the life of God in fellowship with the life of man; the life of man in fellowship with the life of God. That God is our Father, and all men brothers and his children, was the substance of Christ's teaching. The realization of this apostolic Christianity carries in itself the future of human history, and is the solution of all the problems of society.

Many run to and fro with panaceas, which

they think will adjust the inequalities of society and hush the cries of discontent. While many of the proposals are wise and needful, springing from pure desires to help the world to a better condition, yet no political legislation has power, or ever can have power, to make men unselfish. Until men dedicate themselves to lives of unselfishness, and live to do good to all their brothers, and are ready to be as fertile and persevering in labors which are to benefit society as a whole rather than themselves as individuals, injustice and inequality will be banished in one form only to return in some form more seductive and cruel. Until the eternal law of love is written on human hearts, and giving rather than getting inspires the energies of men, and serving rather than being served is received as the joy of life, the best of state legislation is helpless to effect social justice and industrial peace. So long as men are foolish enough to have more faith in the efficacy of law than in the practicability of love, the blood of Abel will continue to cry from the ground. The brand of Cain will rest upon society so long as self-interest is assumed as the social and economic motive. Until the peace of God has fixed the faith of the world on Jesus Christ as the goal of history, and the solvent of all human ills, clasping the hands of men about the cross of Christ — the sign of self-renunciation — as the only law which can establish permanent order and perfect peace, mutual trust and everlasting brotherhood, there will be dissatisfaction and sorrow, injustice and cruelty, despoiling the garden of the Lord. Were it not that Jesus had walked the soil of the earth, re-dedicating it to God, living his divine life amidst the most unfavorable surroundings, I should dwell in absolute hopelessness. But because that life was lived and that death was died, revealing God's attitude towards man, and showing what the life of man may be when it values character above all material things, and believes in love more than food and raiment, I hope all things and believe all things for man. I look for a brotherhood of divine love upon the earth, because Christ is our elder brother, and we shall be like him.

And it is brotherhood, fellowship, which man wants. Brotherhood men will have. The solidarity of the race is impressing itself on the world as the stupendous human fact. Men are feeling about for oneness with each other, as well as for oneness with God. There is a divine impulse, gathering in force with the increase of human sympathy and understanding, which is bearing men on to a larger fellowship with one another. There is a feeling abroad in the world that rivalry and distrust, competition and covetousness, are not the natural, but the un-unnatural, conditions of human society. Men were made to stand together. Social separation is disruption, profanity, damnation, and death. Without brotherhood men cannot endure life, nor its conflicts. Anything that keeps men apart is the work of an enemy to our humanity. The stratification of society is a device of the devil, the slanderer of God, and tempter of man. Social separation, the isolation of the privileged from the unprivileged classes, the withdrawal of life from fellowship with life for material and selfish reasons, is moral anarchy and outrage; it is the most godless and wicked of all infidelity, asserting that human life consists in the abundance of the things which it hath, that the immortal life which God has breathed into man is cheaper than the fashion of his clothes, or worthy of less consideration than the etiquette of his manners. Selfishness as the law of society is hell on earth. The social theory that we are privileged to choose our neighbors is a rending of the body of God by the violence of selfishness; a profanation of God's holy temple, which man is; a condition which will not always be endured. There is no more deadly assumption ever made than the one that money gives any man the right to be unmindful of the interests and needs and feelings of his brother-men. It is the separation of the educated from the ignorant, the rich from the poor, that makes money a root of social evil. All social caste, however ancient and proud, is pagan and evil, hateful and profane. The place of the strong is among the weak, bearing their burdens, enduring the pain and shame of their weakness. The place of the cultured is among the rude and ignorant, lifting them up, teaching them knowledge and goodness and truth. The place of the rich is in living side by side with the poor, not in isolating themselves on separate streets, and not in holding themselves aloof from the company of the poor. The place of those who have is with those who have not, treating them with respect and honor and love that is due unto the children of God. When thou makest a dinner, or a party, call not merely thy rich and congenial friends, who can reward thee with pleasure and return invitations, but invite the poor and ignorant, and even the vicious. This is the gospel of the Son of God, who dwelt among us in our moral rags and poverty, and gave unto us all the glory and wealth of his infinite life. The mere fact that society would regard Christ's social instructions as preposterous, if expected to actually obey them, shows how little our so-called Christian society really knows of Christianity, and how much is yet to be done before we have a society that shall be Christian in reality.

Brotherhood men will have. The movement of the world is in this direction. And it will be a fellowship of truth or a fellowship of sin; a fellowship of love or a fellowship of hate and rapine; a fellowship of atheism or of the church of Christ. In some form or other men will come together, and life will entwine about life, soul will wrap itself about soul, heart will fasten itself to heart, and men will stand together in some great social upheaval and reconstruction. And I believe that in the lead of the social conflict will be found the Son of man, bringing forth a divine social order and establishing a brotherhood of love, showing men that the strength of life is in sacrifice, the joy of life in loving, the enthusiasm of life in serving.

The open door of opportunity which Christ sets before us each to enter is this coming brotherhood of man. To make the love of Christ the foundation of commerce and culture, to make the practice and spread of Christ's quality of love the business of life, is the work to which we are called. Before every human enterprise, before every joy and sorrow, at the first hour and the eleventh, the Son of man sets this clear, strong, eternal motive — a motive that will give a changeless meaning to all human endeavor, making the years a progress to a divine end, linking deed with deed, connecting thought with thought. That men may learn to love and trust one another as the common and redeemed children of the same Father is the reason for the earth's standing through all its storm of sin and shame. It is the purpose with which God began the life of man, and the hope which has sustained man through all the weary ages of his pilgrimage. It is the vision which Christ followed through the wilderness, into Gethsemane, across Calvary, into the clouds. It is the one thing certain in which a man may invest his life and be sure of an eternal return. It is the enterprise in which the living and working Christ would have us be his fellow-workmen. Our stores and factories, our knowledge and culture, our schools and feasts, are opportunities to obey and enforce the commandment to love one another in the life-giving and self-renounced way in which Jesus loved his disciples. The joy of dying that others might live, the glory of living without self-concern, the enthusiasm of feeding his life away to his hungry brothers, — this was the joy that was set before Christ, and is the quenchless joy before us set. To get men to love one another, and thus get the will of God done on earth as it is in heaven, is our mission as truly as it was the mission of Jesus. We can each take this mission as our life-motive — the motive which abides in the heart of God — and keep this motive as the seed of life through all joy and sorrow, success and disappointment, failure and victory. Upon the altar of this infinite purpose we may each dedicate ourselves as living sacrifices, holy and acceptable unto God.

Does this seem a dream? Well, until men believe in the authority of this dream, and proceed to make it the substantial basis of society, the earth will find no rest from woe and war and want. There is salvation from unrest and strife, inequality and injustice, only in simple obedience to Christ's law of love.

However much we may do to procure larger justice through purer laws, until we clasp hands about the cross and agree to take that cross as the law of life, we spend our strength for that which is not eternal bread, and waste our moral resources in playing with the urgent opportunities of Christendom.

The discord and sorrow of sin is the witness that sin is not man's natural condition. Moral weakness is not man's normal state. Evil is an intruder, and has no right in the life of man, nor in God's world. Selfishness is an unnatural outrage upon our humanity. The laws of the devil are not more practicable than the laws of God, neither in the closet nor in the market. Communion with God is man's only natural condition; it is the only use to which time and property can be rightly put. Man is an aimless and wandering prodigal outside of the secret place of the Most High. Humanity at its worst, through all its inexplicable sorrows, along the darkest labyrinths of its sad pilgrimage, has never lost sight of this goal of an endless, sinless, deathless day of peace, in which the presence of God would be the life and light of the world. The race has never been without some eyes pure enough to see a new earth. All prophecy and revelation, the purest statesmanship and best political wisdom, the noblest philosophy and most undefiled religion, have all had this vision of a new earth wherein dwelleth righteousness as their inspiration.

The day of God will come, and the heart of the earth will ache no more, and the riven side of the race will cease to flow, and the spirit of Jesus will be the omnipotent bond of human brotherhood, and children will be born into an atmosphere of prayer, and sin and death be a dream of a night, and the pain of the groaning creation be changed to an anthem of praise, when the disciples of Christ come to so believe in the reality of his redemption that they dedicate all they are and have to the righteousness of his kingdom. The creation groans and travails in pain, waiting only for the children of men to stand forth and show themselves the sons of God.

The day of God will come ; and there will be

night no more. Humanity moves upward; and the heavens lower bend, age by age, folding the earth closer in the heart of the Father. And heaven and earth, under the hand of the risen Christ, who holds the key to human history, will be attuned in one eternal harmony of love. This is the pledge of the cross, and the power of the resurrection. It is the coming kingdom of our Father, which he will receive from the hand of his conquering Christ. And whether we be absent or present, we may work with our Lord in this kingdom which cannot be shaken. Wherefore, let us be steadfast, unmovable, always abounding in the work of the Lord, inasmuch as we know that our labor is not in vain.

III.

THE REALITY OF FAITH.

In England, as elsewhere, the ecclesiastical body still seemed imposing from the memories of its past, its immense wealth, its tradition of statesmanship, its long association with the intellectual and religious aspirations of men, its hold on social life. But its real power was small. Its moral inertness, its lack of spiritual enthusiasm, gave it less and less hold on the religious minds of the day. Its energies, indeed, seemed absorbed in a mere clinging to existence. . . . Its most fatal effect was to rob the priesthood of moral power. Taunted with a love of wealth, with a lower standard of life than that of the ploughman and weaver who gathered to read the Bible by night, dreading in themselves any burst of emotion or enthusiasm as a possible prelude to heresy, the clergy ceased to be the moral leaders of the nation. — *John Richard Green, on the religious condition of England in the fifteenth century.*

It may be that too much time has been spent upon speculations about Christianity, whether true or false, and that that which is essential consists not of speculations, but of facts, and not in technical accuracy on questions of metaphysics, but in the attitude of mind in which we regard them. It would be a cold world in which no sun shone until the inhabitants thereof had arrived at a true chemical analysis of sunlight. And it may be that the knowledge and thought of our time, which is drawing us away from the speculative elements in religion to that conception of it which builds it upon the character and not upon the intellect, is drawing us thereby to that conception of it which the life of Christ was intended to set forth, and which will yet regenerate the world. — *Dr. Edwin Hatch.*

Never was there a time, in the history of the world, when moral heroes were more needed. The world waits for such. The providence of God has commanded science to labor and prepare the way for such. For them she is laying her iron tracks and stretching her wires, and bridging the oceans. But where are they? Who shall breathe into our civil and political relations the breath of a higher life? — *Dr. Mark Hopkins.*

THE REALITY OF FAITH.

And Abraham believed God, and it was reckoned to him for righteousness. — ROM. iv. 3.

THE students of antiquities, reading for us the records of the past on broken bricks and crumbling monuments, say that the times we used to call the dawn of history were, in fact, the noontide of a splendid material development and a vast civilization. Historic science finds no time when the peopled earth has not supported organized institutions, and been crowned by majestic temples. Back of Abraham's time history recedes in the fall and rise of empires; in the decay and growth of religions; in the westward movements of races. In the day that God called Abraham the early Chaldean nations had already taken on some of the magnificence which, centuries hence, was to make the kingdom of Nebuchadnezzar the very exaggeration of Oriental genius and power. Ur, from whence Abraham went forth obedient to the divine command to found a new nation, was a strong-walled city of astronomers and poets, politics and trades, soldiers and libraries, theatres and temples.

But this ancient civilization was a beautiful and gigantic body without a soul. It knew much of force, but little of law; something of beauty, but nearly nothing of morals. It celebrated the vilest sins as religious rites. It was built upon faith in the seen, in ignorance of the unseen realities. And the Chaldeans, making the mistake which has been fatal to the permanence of all civilizations, believed in their luxury and material prosperity as progress. They were immensely satisfied with themselves, and proud of their achievements. Some of their expressions of self-approbation, which the scholars have translated for us, are striking in their likeness to the typical American Fourth of July oration, though made from three to four thousand years ago. Blind and fallen human nature, tempted from God by the serpent of covetousness, has always spent its strength and skill on the husks and clothes of life, while the substance dissolved in glorious corruption. Civilizations have always been shorn of their strength in the lap of luxury, their decay shrouded in material grandeur. Wealth is progress only when it is a communion with God and a bond of brotherhood between men. The spirit of wealth has never dominated a civilization and dictated its laws, save to its ultimate destruction.

Amidst the might and luxury of the primitive Chaldean world lived a man who had kept himself free from its sensuous idolatry, and pure enough to see one of God's beckoning stars of promise; so he decided to cast in his lot with God. Abraham could not have been unacquainted with the material grandeur of this Oriental civilization; but he was not corrupted by its grossness, nor dazzled by its splendor. He began to have fitful dreams of a new and better order of things upon the earth. He could not believe that God was any the better satisfied with falsehood and cruelty, lust and luxury, because they were housed in huge palaces and clothed in silk and gold. As he brooded over the magnificent wretchedness of his times, and watched God's star of promise shining from the future, there was borne in upon him a strong impulse to move out into the world in the hope of establishing a nation that would be the seed of a new earth. That impulse bade him get away from the corrupt civilization wherein he dwelt, into a westward land which he had never seen, and there raise up unto his God a new people. He accepted that impulse as the voice of God. He gave into his divine instincts implicit obedience. He believed God, and it was reckoned unto him for righteousness. And through all the lonely and eventful years that followed, as he pilgrimaged to and fro across the promised land, he followed the voice that spake in the secret places of his soul. When God promised him a son in his old age, he believed God in this as in everything else, and it was reckoned unto him for righteousness. And when we consider Abraham's times, their social and religious condition, it is no wonder he comes down to us as the most illustrious ancient hero of faith.

What, now, is the faith that moves prophetic souls out of the beaten walks of life, and up the higher walks, where a reluctant race slowly follows them? What is the nature of the faith which makes for righteousness? What is the essence, the reality, of faith? What is it, in our times, that makes one man's belief in God a religious pleasantry and social propriety, and another man's faith a creative force in society?

Faith does not consist in holding correct opinions of God. Dr. Martineau truly says that "nothing so marks the degradation of modern Christianity as the notion that faith is only opinion." A man may hold the most proper opinions of God, he may believe in every letter of the most orthodox confession of faith, and be a graceful infidel in all his thought, an atheist in all his practices. Probably all that Abraham knew of God was that he stood for righteousness against unrighteousness; but to that knowledge Abraham surrendered himself, with all that he possessed. God cares nothing for a man's opinions of himself, or his attributes, when the man's moral aspirations reach not beyond a respectable social and financial standing on earth, and a comfortable mansion in heaven. Opinion is not faith.

Nor is faith a substitute for righteousness. The conception of faith as something God accepts in the place of holiness is a Protestant superstition as unscriptural and immoral as any superstition of middle-age Catholicism. The assumption that men can lead selfish and covetous lives, and then reach heaven by believing the right things about God, needs to be eliminated from the religious thought of the church of our day as surely as the sale of indulgences from the church of Luther's day. The church will never take up its divinely appointed task of righting the wrong things of this world until it comes to thoroughly understand that Christ came not to save men in their sins, but to give them power to cease from all ungodliness. There is no salvation from sin other than the abandonment of sin, neither in this world nor the world to come. Opinions of God are no magic to change character at death. He that is unrighteous before death will be unrighteous still; he that is unjust will still be unjust; the selfish man will still be selfish. A man is not justified by faith unless faith has made him just. He may have the greatest respect for God, be extremely polite in his treatment of God, attentive to all divine ordinances, thinking he doeth God service as a protector of faith, and yet be destitute of all knowledge of the reality of faith, barren of any moral conception of what it means to believe God.

Faith is that response of the will of man which unites it to the will of God. Faith is that step, whether one or many, which conjoins the life of a man with the life of God. Faith is that action which surrenders all one's interests to the getting of God's will done upon the earth as it is done in heaven. Faith is unreserved co-operation, partnership, friendship with God, so that God possesses the life, working with it and through it; so that the man of faith is not his own man, but God's man. The man of faith is not blinded by the self-satisfaction of society; not deceived by material progress; neither bewildered by the babble of admiring voices, nor borne down beneath defeat. It is the very essence of faith to listen only to the voice of God, and learn what God wants done and is doing in the believer's day and generation, inquiring not for immediate results, conscious that only righteousness is progressive and profitable in the everlasting summing-up of things. He who believes God asks himself if God be satisfied with the state of things in his age; in his country or city; in his church or his own heart. Listening eagerly to the voice that speaks in the secret place of his conscience, he peers into the future for stars of promise, and obeys the inspirations of hope borne in upon him in the solitude of prayer. Then, having seen what God is doing in the opportunities and questions of his day, he gives himself with utter self-abandon to working the work of God. He knows that God can will nothing but the best; so he tolerates nothing in himself but the highest ideals of duty and character. He doubts not that the righteous will of God must ultimately prevail, and joyously endures temporal losses for righteousness' sake. If he must lose the comfort and civilization of Ur of Chaldea, he fears not that God will provide something better than Ur for himself and his children. So he casts in his lot with God, without asking to know what that lot may be.

Hence the man of faith does not ask what is the safe course for him to take. He who seeks to do no more than what is considered safe, even in a religious way, is destitute of the power of faith. He may, in a sense, be a good man, beautiful in many attributes of character; but he is not among those who put to flight the armies of aliens, and quench the fires of wickedness, and work the constructive righteousness of God into the fabrics of history. No man has faith to succeed in any cause who is not ready to face worldly failure, and endure the defeat of his cause; willing even to find himself mistaken, if he may thereby get at the heart of the eternal realities.

He may be a man imperfect, not so fair to look upon as the man at his side who walks by calculation and sight, but yet a man whose belief in God allows him to make no terms with his imperfections. He sees great gaps between his faith and his practice, and is agonized with the shame of his weakness. Torn with vain climbing; sick with baffled effort; gaining a little here, and there backward swept by sudden passion; mangled upon the rocks of pride, from which gush no healing springs of sympathy; the soul of faith yet presses on, undismayed by failure, fearing no foes. He has more faith in the power of God than in the impotence of his own weakness. He has given himself into the keeping of the will of God, and knows that goodness alone will endure in his life at last, if he let God keep him.

Thus it is not by faith in his own poor power that the lonely prophet of faith moves out from the trodden paths of life and thought, from the midst of a conceited civilization, in a self-satisfied age without a spiritual vision; but by faith in the omnipotent reign of the redeeming Lord God. Not because he feels himself better than others — he may know himself as the chief of sinners — does the man of faith throw down the gauntlet of challenge before the time-honored walls of sin, and bid their jeering hosts a joyous defiance; but because he feels the grasp of the Almighty hand upon his life, and hears the commanding whisper of the eternal Word in his soul. An overmastering consciousness of God, swallowing up the sense of weakness and all self-consciousness, makes his belief forceful amidst the forceless and unvital religious conventionalism that sits in self-appointed judgment on his words and work. God is with him, working with his hands, walking on his feet, pouring infinite thoughts into his brain, speaking with his mouth, loving with his heart, possessing and empowering all his faculties, directing all his energies. It is this tremendous conviction that he is working with God, that God has moved in and pitched his tent in his soul, that makes a man's belief count for righteousness. It is this that enables God to stake the eternal interests of his kingdom on the faith of some poor and sinful human soul. It is this that lifts hands of faith to reach across the ages and make the moral wealth of the future the inheritance of the present. This it is that makes wise saints of illiterate sinners, while cultured religionists stand dumb and ashamed. This it is that calls forth praises from the mouths of babes in knowledge, while its masters stare in unsympathetic wonderment. By this faith the weak things of the world bring low the things that are strong, and the blundering enthusiast does the mighty work of God, while prudent conservatism declares him a destroyer of religion. The consciousness of God is the power of faith, and surrender to God is its essence. Faith is the source of all righteousness, and righteousness alone can be its fruit. For nothing but righteousness can faith be reckoned to any soul. Faith is itself the absolute righteousness. Men are as great and righteous in the eternal course of things as their faith. Righteousness is wrought in the world by men whose lives are one condensed belief in God.

Abraham believed God; and his faith is bearing fruit in earth-wide and eternal harvests of righteousness, filling the earth with the knowledge of the Lord as the waters cover the sea. Moses believed God; and his belief is yet fashioning human institutions after the mind of God. Elijah believed God; and in the secret of Elijah's praying-places God formed new epochs of history. David believed God; and the Spirit breathed into his sinful soul celestial songs of deathless hopes. Daniel believed God; and by the hand of the captive Jew God started the earth upon a new career. Paul believed God; and watch him as he goes from nation to nation, striding the earth like the moral colossus that he is; before his advance the work of armies is undone, walls of partition crumble between man and man, gates of brass swing open, thrones topple, and a new Europe leaps from the ruins Rome has wrought of a race's liberties. John believed God; and down into his self-emptied soul was poured the fulness of God's mind, so that he writes the words of God to centuries far distant, and writes as never the pen of man has written. Calvin, the timid scholar, believed God; and God made him the bulwark of freedom against which the wrath of unrighteousness and the judgments of hypocrisy could not prevail. Cromwell believed God; and look at him, a pious and wrathful English farmer, muttering against tyranny and popery, brooding over his Bible while sin revels in church and rules the state. While he prays and grumbles, somehow God's omnipotence gets down inside of that farmer, and when he girds on his sword for his dreadful work, the earth quakes beneath his tread, and hell is helpless to stop him; he makes the Anglo-Saxon with his Bible the master of the world. Edwards, the metaphysician and poet, believed God; and the awakened church put on new garments of life that now shine into the uttermost islands of the sea. And what shall I say more? Time would fail me to tell of Luther and Wesley; of England's Alfred and America's Lincoln; of a great multitude whom only God had noted, who through great tribulation, through sorrow and shedding of blood, have by faith wrought righteousness, subdued kingdoms, obtained promises, out of weakness been made strong. Great hosts of unnamed witnesses, of whom the world was not worthy, adjure us to run with patience the race of faith that is set before us, looking unto Jesus, the author and perfecter of our faith, who for the joy of doing the will of God and serving his brethren endured the cross of self-renunciation, despised the shame of worldly failure, and now sits on the right hand of our Father's glory.

There has been no day in Christian history which offered the opportunity for heroism of faith that Christ sets before our day and church. In no age of redemption has our Christ called so urgently for men who believe God. We live in a time of unbelief; not unbelief in the existence of God; not unbelief in the fact of religion; but unbelief in the practicability of righteousness. Theology presumes that righteousness cannot be actualized upon the earth. The church does not believe that men can do as the Lord Jesus tells them. The society that calls itself Christian believes in neither the wisdom nor the authority of the Sermon on the Mount. The notion that God will accept opinion in the place of obedience is the strong delusion that is leading Christendom into living a stupendous lie. Unbelief in righteousness is the most vicious unbelief in God. To suppose that God can be satisfied with less than his own goodness in humanity is to suppose God less than perfectly good himself. To proceed with human life on the presumption that the gospel of God commands us to be and do what is impossible is the most fatal infidelity the church has ever had to meet; and it meets it within its own precincts. The cherishing of low ideals of duty and character is the very substance of unbelief. There is no atheism so frightful in its consequences to the age, so troublesome to the throne of God, so anarchical an element in the universe, as the conclusion that Christliness of character is inconsistent with the management of the earthly affairs of man. It would be better in the sight of God that every creed should become a scandal, and every house of worship a heap of ruins, than that men should accept selfishness as the law of human activities. For God is able to enter doors of faith, to fill the innermost recesses of our being, and master the minutest details of our activities, and glorify himself in all we think and do. It is because unbelief closes these doors of faith that the earth has waited so long and sadly for God to dwell with man in unbroken communion, making the race his untroubled people. It can be through naught but unbelief that the church of Christ shall fail to lead the sons of men into the promised land of brotherhood, now beckoning the church to a new career and undreamed-of triumph.

We are in the early beginnings of a reconstructive epoch. The light of a great day of God is breaking upon the hill-tops of faith, and streaking the social horizon, and piercing the gloom of want which sits long and heavy upon the valleys of toil. There is a feeling abroad in the world, daily deepening into an impatient conviction, that Christ is pressing upon a reluctant church the key of love that can unlock the problems of society. The prophetic hearts of our age, broken with a great hope for man which could find no response in rationalistic orthodoxy, are turning anew to the living

Christ of the Gospels, and are rejoicing in the healing touch of his sympathy. The race is grasping a thought of redemption which means righteousness and peace, justice and brotherhood, and the bearing of the burdens of the weak by the strong. Without the temple wait the multitudes, eager to crown the slain Christ whom the scribes and Pharisees may again cast out, and follow him even unto death in the victory of faith that overcometh the world.

When I meet the sin of the world in its most woful forms; when I marvel at our blind and growing faith in money as the solvent of earth's ills; when I speak to the deaf ears of religious pride, and behold a nation mistaking steam whistles and opera houses for progress, and towering temples of trade and palaces of domestic luxury for national prosperity; when I see the smiling indifference of the fashionable few who cluster about the splendid churches, while the great unloved peoples, daily growing in numbers and poverty and vice, are asking fateful questions about right and wrong which the church does not answer; when I see the Almighty hand gathering lightnings of destruction in the heavens to let loose upon the strongholds of mammon;— then a strong agony cries out in my soul for men who believe God. Be they soever poor and ignorant, sinful and obscure, let me clasp hands, O God, with men who discern the signs of the times; men who see thy beckoning stars of promise, who hear something of what thou art saying to this material-loving age, who rejoice to cast in their lot with thee, sharing in the sorrow and glory of fulfilling thy righteousness! Up and down the world of strife and work the Christ of judgment is moving, appealing for hearts that do believe that the will of God may yet be done on earth as it is done in heaven. He calls for men who are willing to endure the loss of money and fling reputation to the winds, that they may work with God for the creation of a Christian society and a heavenly civilization.

The straightening-out of the social ills of the world could be speedily accomplished, if men who profess the gospel would take the mission of establishing the market on a gospel foundation as a serious and practicable mission. It is a sheer want of faith that keeps this sublime work from being done in the name of the Lord Jesus. If the Christian business men of our day, who know the gospel and know the commands of our Lord, would take it as the purpose of their lives to make all their business relations a revelation of the practicability of the gospel, dealing with their fellow-men according to the gospel rule of doing to others as if they themselves were the others; if they would take hold of this great determination to Christianize the business of the world, and make brothers of men, with the equally strong determination never to let go, come what may;—then they could work the greatest reform, they could bring in the divinest era, ever known to history. If there were a thousand souls ready to fling themselves, like Abraham, upon the tides of their divinest instincts, without asking to see whither they would bear them, and follow Christ in the deep and wide sense of the apostles, there would be such a heaving-up of this world as would lift the loftiest ranges of its life into the skies; and the warrior angels of Christ would descend to join the climbing saints in battle for the everlasting triumph of righteousness.

I understand that, looking at the matter of absolute self-dedication to the work of God in one way, there seems little encouragement to inspire the single life. Every social and religious convulsion that has destroyed the old and brought forth a new earth has crushed and buried the prophets of the better day. The world has always mocked the faces which brightest shone with new revelations of truth, and pierced the hands that came to it laden with God's new gifts of life. Idle seems the dream of social righteousness to so large a part of those who name Christ as their Redeemer, while with cynical indifference the bloody feet of covetousness tramp on their way of woe. The amazing moral ignorance of the rich sickens us with the sad intellectual ignorance of the poor. Hypocrisy and injustice and despotism seem to die only for a resurrection in some finer and more deceptive form. By none is the actual kingdom of Christ more bitterly antagonized than the zealous religious classes, while, —

> "Still on the highroad, 'neath the noon-day sun,
> The fires of hate are lit for those who dare
> Follow their Lord along the untrodden way."

Of small power seems a single life of self-denial amidst the wide and desolate wastes of selfishness. What can a few souls, confronting a great infidel church supremely anxious to keep on good terms with the world and conserve the traditions of the elders, — what can they do to give the gospel back to men? And the doubt is intensified by the delay that hopes for some organization to arise to do the work which only consecrated hearts and loving hands and sacrificial lives can do. The Roman trust in comprehensive organization and Anglo-Saxon faith in the opinion of majorities have obscured from the eyes of our American Christianity the majestic simplicity of the gospel methods of our Lord.

The kingdom has always come through the

faith of the consecrated few. Great institutions and organizations have nearly always come to plant themselves squarely across the march of the divine purposes. By the consecration of single souls, and small groups of souls, has righteousness been increasing with the ages. By the few listening spirits have God's great thoughts been spoken; and the few obedient lives have wrought the heavenly doing of his will in the earth's epochal hours. The race has entered its holier eras of wider freedom and purer justice at the heels of humble and patient souls whom it scoffed while it followed. It is the majesty of simple goodness in single characters that reveals God in converting and conquering power to the world. By no other organization than the fellowship which each man finds while walking the path of obedience to the will of God can the world be altogether overcome, and the dream of world-wide brotherhood become an eternal fact. "If the single man," says Emerson, speaking according to the gospel, "plant himself indomitably upon his divine instincts, and there abide, the huge world will come round to him."

We none of us need wait, in this day of human need and divine judgment, for company and organization. We need no program of action save the words of our Lord, sending us, as he was sent by the Father, to please not ourselves, but give our lives as bread and meat to a hungry world. There is no thinking, no estimating, here, what the most infirm and fettered of us each may be and do for God and man if we but make of ourselves living sacrifices in his service, to be conformed to Christ and not the opinions and customs of time. We may each, acting with the apostolic faith in the power of love and truth, pentecosted with the apostolic enthusiasm for righteousness, send out divine influences that will submerge vast intrenchments of evil and bear the race far Godward in their sweep. If we but put faith in the noiseless voice that speaks in the deeps of our being, rather than the lifeless artificialities of society and the hard selfishness of the market, we may translate the divinest ideals of life and conduct into common-place realities. If we trust the light within us more than the darkness without us, our holiest dreams may become the most substantial facts of our experience. The Christ who calls us to enter and share his life and work with God is himself the power by which we overcome the evil of the world, and face the scorn of its bruising customs. Arise, let us go hence to cast our crowns at the feet of the sovereign Christ and share in the toil and tribulation, the patience and triumph, of his coming kingdom. And he will write upon us his own name, and make us pillars in the earth-enclosing temple of love, which is the new Jerusalem coming down out of heaven from God.

IV.

THE FAITH THAT OVERCOMETH THE WORLD.

IT has been sometimes said of late years that Christianity has resigned the leadership of the world, and that the friends of humanity must now step in to act as a natural Providence and conduct the affairs of the race. There is some truth in the complaint, whatever we may think of the proposed remedy. For there has been at all times a tendency among Christians to abandon the claim of universal sovereignty which was at first made in the name of the Lord. The claim may be made in words, but left in a purely ideal state ; and when no attempt has been made to give it a practical application, it is in effect abandoned. A Christianity which embraces a part of human life, while it adjourns its fuller claim to the world beyond the grave, is certainly not the religion of One who says, "All power is given unto me in heaven and in earth." — *Canon Fremantle.*

Religion does not permeate life. The Church is one of the great institutions of the country, and gets its own place. But it is a thing apart from the common life, which goes on beside it. Business, politics, literature, amusements, are only faintly colored by it. Yet the mission of Christianity is not to occupy a respectable place apart, but to leaven life through and through. — *Dr. James Stalker.*

In fact, the godless lover of gain, and the gainless lover of God are fanatics both, taking hold of the opposite ends of the same falsehood. And the truth which suffices to rebuke them both is this: that the kingdom of God is not a business, set up in rivalry with worldly business; but a divine law regulating, and a divine temper pervading, the pursuits of worldly business. — *Dr. James Martineau.*

There is but one thing needful — to possess God. All our senses, all our powers of mind and soul, all our external resources, are so many ways of approaching the divinity, so many modes of tasting and adoring God. We must learn to detach ourselves from all that is capable of being lost; to bind ourselves absolutely only to what is absolute and eternal, and to enjoy the rest as a loan. — *Amiel's Journal.*

THE FAITH THAT OVERCOMETH THE WORLD.

Who is he that overcometh the world, but he that believeth that Jesus is the Son of God? — 1 JOHN v. 5.

IT was not by reliance on any visible support the apostles went forth to claim the world for Christ. They could count upon no earthly resources. The institutions of man were against them. They were opposed by governments, schools of learning, and established religions. Nothing seemed more foolish and hopeless to the world than the assertion of the kingship of Christ, who left his disciples without an inch of worldly standing-ground, without a thread of earthly dependence to which they could cling. They had no temples of worship; no philosophy, or system of theology; no literature, save some of the books of the Old Testament. They were without social position or political influence, without wealth or the friendship of wealth. The kingdoms of the world and their glory, which had once filled so large a place in the ambitions of the apostles, were a vanished dream when Peter and John began to proclaim the crucified Christ as the living king of heaven and earth. There was never such a congestion of human helplessness as the hundred and twenty men and women who met in that upper chamber at Jerusalem, to wait for the reception of the unseen power that was to make their deeds mighty and their words convincing.

Nor was it by faith in superior intellectual gifts the disciples did their work. Christ left no educated ministry, according to our interpretation of education. Peter and John were unlettered fishermen. And the epistles of Paul show a sublime unconsciousness of the great theological problems which have occupied the scholars of the church. Humanity, and not theology, was the apostolic burden. The change of the centre of Christian thought from the sphere of righteousness to the sphere of metaphysics, coming after the apostles' time, was a corruption of Christianity; a compromise of the gospel with the sceptical philosophy of a pagan world. The fixing of the attention of Christendom upon opinion rather than upon character, the occupation of the Christian intellect with definitions rather than with righteousness, levelled the Christian ministry to the authority of the scribes of traditionalism, whom Christ rebuked with unqualified severity. The putting of theology in the place of life as the object of Christian concern was a victory for the devil, and an utter perversion of the mind of the gospel. The early Christian churches were composed, in the main, of the poor and ignorant. The epistles of the New Testament were written, the greatest of them, to bond-servants. Paul, one of the most accomplished men of all times, speaks with intense distrust of the intellectual graces which were so highly prized in his day, and are so strangely and sadly over-valued in ours. The great apostle felt keenly the degradation of being taken for a mere religious orator. He saw that the centres of culture were seats of refined and shameless vice. John, too, saw the moral stupidity of even the best philosophy. All the apostles fought with the beasts of theological selfishness, and bore the stripes of religious bigotry. They knew the uselessness of contending against the blindness and meanness of the professional religionist, who enthrones the idol of his system in the place of the living God. At one time and another, the apostles also dealt with that moral drivelling which characterizes all mere intellectual culture. Not by the wisdom of the world, religious or philosophical, any more than by the world's institutions, did they expect to win the world to their king. They were no cultivated religious gentlemen, reading the literature of the day and writing proper religious essays in well-appointed studies.

Neither by faith in their own righteousness were they victorious in their labors. They knew they had been childish and selfish, fickle and false. They saw themselves as sinners, along with all mankind. They felt in fellowship with the most wretched and fallen. They regarded themselves as miracles of mercy. Continued self-acquaintance only increased their self-abasement, and their wonder at the gracious love that saved them. Not because they thought themselves better than other men were they enabled and encouraged to go as ambassadors of righteousness and truth to the nations. Better than any of us, I fear, they felt the waste and weakness of sin. Through great sinning and great suffering they learned the lessons of redemption.

The faith by which the apostles overcame the world was in their acceptance of the absolute authority of Jesus Christ over all human life. In the faith that God had revealed himself in Christ as a deliverer from every form of sin they toiled in the divine might of a redeemed manhood. By faith in Christ as the manifested power and revealed wisdom of God they cut loose from bondage to the past, and swung clear of dependence on visible supports and earthly resources. To them God was no condescending Christless infinity, but a heavenly Father who had shown forth his entire character and spoken his whole word in Christ. In the light and joy of this revelation they suffered and worked with Christ as the conqueror of all things visible and invisible. They were the devoted subjects of a king who was making a new earth in which he would reign in righteousness. The race was redeemed; sin had no more right to dominion over men; since the revelation of God in Christ there was no more excuse for abiding in unrighteousness. Christ had overcome the world; to him the nations belonged; his Spirit was subjecting them unto God; he was the ruler of the kings of earth — the apostles were the proclaimers of this fact. To the apostles redemption was a reality. There was in the coming of Christ an influx of moral power sufficient to deliver the world from all wickedness, making covetousness and selfishness, lust and strife, unnecessary. In the faith that Christ who had been slain was living and reigning, that he was surely conquering the world for the Father who had given it into his hands, the apostles were bold and tireless in announcing the fact that the world was redeemed from the power, not the consequences, of sin. They believed they were fighting the good fight of a victorious Christ, and that henceforth human history would be the realization of the fruits of his redemption in the establishment of his everlasting kingdom. Under the kingship of the Christ of all grace and truth, righteousness was no longer an experiment; human life was a triumph, and not a defeat; right and wrong were not problems; the world was redeemed with a complete redemption; only unbelief could regard any sin, personal or social, as irremovable.

It was thus impossible for the apostles to sustain any other relation to the right than that of triumphantly asserting it in the name of their king; or hold any other relation to the wrong than that of smiting it by the same authority. They were not engaged in any doubtful struggle. They could conceive of no possibility of defeat. They were the followers of one before whom nothing could stand. They never considered that the issue of their labors and sorrows, their prayers and faith, could be less than the subjection of all human life to the rule of Christ. From the day his Spirit armed them for service they maintained an unchanging attitude of triumph. An unbroken strain of victory is borne along from apostle to apostle through the writings of the New Testament. They attacked the world as men who were victors from the outset. In the faith that the uplifting of Christ was the mortal blow to the dominion of Satan; that the resurrection of Christ revealed death as a gain and not a loss; that the coming of the Spirit was the spreading forth of the power of Christ to gather all kingdoms and governments, all families and societies, all knowledge and commerce, under the eternal sovereignty of love; — in this faith they toiled and endured as seeing the invisible Christ already on the throne of universal dominion. In this faith they rejoiced in persecutions, and lifted voices of thanksgiving from prison-walls and martyr-fires. They received the blows of the Lord's enemies in the faith that every blow weakened the power of evil and hastened the world's deliverance. They believed that the truth which the world rejected in them as falsehood would be welcomed by ages to come as a precious inheritance. They suffered the loss of all things that coming generations might be enriched by faith's sacrifices. They were blinded by no blasphemous separation of the world into secular and spiritual spheres; fettered by no restrictions of the power of Christ's redemptive grace or the authority of his sovereign love. They had not betrayed Christ to philosophers by abandoning the gospel for systems of theology; nor exchanged the weapons of faith and love for the kingdoms of the world and their glory. They dared not think of any evil under the sun as other than a defeated alien, a retreating enemy. Faith in Christ as immanent and sovereign in all human affairs, not faith in any power in themselves, not faith in the favors or resources of the world, was the might by which the apostles worked out the salvation of a redeemed race. By no other quality of faith can the church overcome the world.

Sometimes I ask myself whether the Son of man, as he comes in the crises and opportunities of our age, finds faith in the church — the faith that overcometh the world; the faith that Christ has redeemed the world. The question cannot be answered by the number of Bibles printed and read; for no faith is vital and conquering that depends mainly for its knowledge of God on written records. As Andrew Murray says, "There may be a study and knowledge of the word in which there is but little real fellowship with the living God." Our Father is a God of the living as well as of the dead. He is not dumb nor speechless, save to unbelief. Inspiration is quenchless, revelation continuous. Nor can the quality and quantity of faith be measured by the number and beauty of our churches. God dwelleth not alone in temples made with hands. There cometh in Christ one greater than our temples of material splendor, which are monuments to human pride quite as much as to a living faith. We all know, if we are candid, that some magnificent temples of worship are built to shut out rather than gather in the lost sheep of the house of Israel. Social caste has, in too many instances, more to do with the erection of palaces of worship than faith in Christ. And God cares not for churches which have not in them the mind which was in Christ Jesus. There is a wide distinction to be made between religious respectability and the love for humanity which is the spirit and power of the gospel. Christ does not measure a church's faith by the beauty of its adornments, nor the ecclesiastical prominence of its preacher, but by the attitude of the church towards a world of sin and need. By love alone can a church vindicate its right to bear the name of the crucified Christ. By this shall all men know that ye are my disciples, if ye have love one to another. Is the church doing the same work that Christ did, its members making themselves of no reputation, and going about doing good in the power of the Holy Spirit? A church has faith only to the degree that the church is Christ to its community. Neither do our creeds evidence the reality of our belief. Opinions about Christ, orthodox or unorthodox, are not faith in Christ. Not in these does the Son of man look for faith.

They are no part of the gospel, and are totally foreign to the spirit of the apostles. No one would have resented them more vehemently than Paul. The cataloguing of God's attributes as the symbol of Christian faith is a triumph of heathen philosophy. Orthodox symbols are often the refuge of the most substantial atheism, the most godless covetousness, and impudent infidelity. And Christianity must be lifted out of the realm of metaphysics and put down again in the realm of morals. The seat of religious judgment must shift from opinion to character. For while the church has busied itself with definitions, throwing itself into panics over supposed intellectual errors, flagrant moral errors and infidel practices have grown up under the protection of the most pretentious orthodoxy. While distracting itself over the unknown program of moral procedure in another world, the church has practically abandoned the ethics of the Sermon on the Mount, which is God's program of moral procedure in this. Nor yet the mere number of religious industries, or benevolent activities, or charitable endowments, which we record, can in themselves prove our faith. They may be objects of faith and worship rather than the living God. There is a measureless amount of religious activity and churchliness which is not Christian, and has no vital relation to the gospel. "This is the work of God, that ye believe on him whom he hath sent." There is also a vast deal of modern benevolence, flattering indeed to a world-won church, which is nothing less than a hard-hearted apology for cruelty, extortion, and robbery.

Our Christian faith can be measured only by the quality of our self-surrender. No faith is vital which does not supply itself with virtue. That faith is a fiction which does not fruit in self-sacrifice and righteousness. We believe in Christ just to the measure we give ourselves up to him, walking in his way of life, guided by his truth, obeying his law of love, going about doing good in the spirit and power of his holiness. It is the faith that leaves one no more his own man, but Christ's man; the faith that puts no conditions in the surrender of self to the mastership of Christ; the faith that counts temporal losses as eternal gains, that it may know Christ and live his life; the faith that rests not upon the friendship of the world, nor upon any formula of truth, but on Christ as the power and wisdom of God; the faith that conforms the life to Christ, and not to the fashions of social selfishness; the faith that nails the whole being in grateful self-surrender on the cross of the slain Christ. Faith never reaches far beyond self-renunciation. And the moment we are self-surrendered to Christ, with all the passions of life attached to him as the supreme object of affection and sacrifice, and the supreme joy of aspiration, that moment we enter the freedom, and share in the life, and work with the strength of God. Life is henceforth a victory. We then work with our eyes on Christ, looking not at self, working most and best when all thoughts of success and failure are absorbed in the faith that Christ has redeemed the world. The soul that is bound to Christ by this faith works on, faithful alike in victory and defeat, knowing that he whose world this is conquers with failure as well as success. It broods not over its own weakness, nor faints at the sorrow of baffled effort ; nor does its energy fail in the presence of strong and confident evils. Through Christ, in Christ, with Christ, it overcomes the world. The Christ-possessed soul walks the world of storms serene and omnipotent, tossed not about upon the waves of opinion, nor distracted by the babble of voices. It has cast its anchor in the secret place of the Most High, the harbor of eternal hope where Jesus is, and abides without fear till the clouds of time shall break from the face of God.

Christ is all that God can make of man. In him is the righteousness of God which is the search of history. In him is the complete manifestation of God's love and power in humanity. By faith in him is the race to be made whole. Not in barren ethical abstractions, which have no ground in reality; not in theological formulas, which are the unbelief of logic ; but in personal devotion to Jesus Christ is the purifying power of the world, and the secret of man's moral development. In the hand of Jesus is the key to human history. Faith in him as the destiny of man and the revelation of the Father is the hope that shall make us perfect as our Father in heaven is perfect. The race will advance in righteousness, and enter its eternal rest from strife, as fast and fully as it accepts Christ as ruler. Nothing greater than Christ, neither in institutions nor in doctrines, can man think for personal guidance or social law. When the earth yields allegiance to the law of love in Christ it will be Eden-clad again. The spirit of Christ must be the spirit of commerce, of politics, of society. The complete reformation of the world, the reconstruction of society, the saving of the Christless multitudes, will come through the acceptance of the mastership of Jesus on the part of the church that bears his name. There are no social problems in fact. They exist only in the imagination of unbelief. Every problem of your life and mine, every problem of government and finance, every problem of capital and labor, will find quick and simple solution when men who call Christ their

Lord are willing to obey his commands. There is not a single question, individual or universal, that cannot find its final and philosophic answer through belief in Jesus as the Son of God and king of men. We have but one thing to do to right the wrongs of the world; and that is, to submit ourselves, in every sphere of life, to the authority of Christ, and exalt him as the King whose right it is to reign in every domain of human activity. By enslavement to Christ is the race to be made free. He is the righteousness for which the world sorrows and waits. He is God's spoken word concerning right and wrong. He is the truth for which wise fools search in vain; the truth which God is raising in a new resurrection from beneath the *débris* of centuries of conflict. When all human life comes to be lived out under the authority of Jesus, it will then be rightly lived. Through union with Christ in God will all the ills of the divine body of humanity be healed. Through the lifting up of the Son of man with our own pierced hands of faith will the race be drawn into the nightless light of the throne of love.

All the power of God unto salvation is in Christ, who has overcome the world and redeemed it unto God, seeing that his divine power hath granted unto us all things that pertain unto life and godliness.

The problems of our times are demanding of the church a larger and more apostolic conception of redemption. The hungry millions without the church, stretching forth worn hands of hope, are beseeching us to know if good be stronger than evil, and love mightier than greed. There is a feeling moving in the world, deepening into a terrible suspicion, that Christ is not fairly represented by his church; that we have been regarding Christ as a Saviour in our sins instead of from our sins. Too long have we been limiting the power of the Son of God in the interests of churchly selfishness and dogmatic theology. The social questions of the day are the notes of God's trumpet calling the church to a new career. The church must answer the call, and manifest Christianity to the world as a divinely human brotherhood, or bring upon itself some terrible judgment that will level its temples to the dust, and make its creeds a derision. It must form a larger estimate of the riches that God has treasured in Christ, waiting to lavish them upon a recipient world.

The world has long heard from theology that it is condemned. The divine fact which needs to be uttered with prophetic emphasis upon the earth in our day is the reality of redemption. Society must be told that there has been given unto men in Christ a power great enough to deliver them from the law of selfishness. Redemption is a fact, and not an imputation or a fiction. The cleansing powers of the blood of Christ are moral and actual. We have no excuse for abiding in unrighteousness. Covetousness is atheism; the supremacy of the law of self-interest is infidelity; social caste is profanity. God forbid that we should continue in these sins any longer, blaspheming God with the delusion that grace may abound through our unrighteousness; for thereby we trample under foot the precious blood of Christ, and neglect to our peril his great salvation. And how can the church escape if it neglects to work out the salvation of Jesus in a regenerated society?

I speak not, my brethren, in the interests of any theology, old or new. I speak in the name of the living Christ, for the sake of the church which bears his name, and for the sake of a travailing earth that waits for us to stand forth and show ourselves to be indeed the sons of God. I feel that we need to free ourselves from all fear of men, and all bondage to human traditionalism, that we may get very low at the feet of the suffering Christ, and ask him to show us what his gospel really is, and what its message is to our day and generation. It is time that judgment begin at the house of God. To be the messengers of judgment will cost us much. But we can afford the cost, if we may do our part towards starting the church upon a career which will restore Christianity to Christendom, and give back the gospel to men. May the Spirit of all holiness and power fill us with that divine discontent which will not let us rest in the pride and injustice of the present order of things, but move us into the future as bearers of the reproach of Christ, and seekers of that coming city of God, whose wall of peace shall enclose the nations and shut out all darkness forever.

In the flashes of divine judgment that rift the clouds which darkly gather on the horizon of the church, beyond the idolatry of a mammon-serving age, through the smoke of speeding conflicts, out of the ashes of dreadful ruins, I see a scourged and purified church returning to the faith of the apostles, its torn and trampled robes stripped of worldly adornments and new-washed in the blood of the slain Lamb. It may be a church of the remnant, desolate and crippled, but a church repentant and triumphant through faith in the Son of God as the ruler of the kings of earth. In that ransomed church, delivered from the kingdoms of the world and their glory, no throne of mammon shall stand beside the cross of the crucified Christ. It will bear the cross about in loving hearts, bleeding with the love of God for fallen men, and lean no more upon fashion and wealth. It will point no more to wordy symbols and material magnificence as the witnesses of its faith, but to lives of Christly righteousness. It will be led by brave souls who will bring their all to the feet of Christ, in the faith that his cross of self-renunciation is the only practicable law of human society. And though the world may mock them as fools, they will overcome through the blood of the Lamb, loving not their lives unto death, and lead the race through the gates of the new Jerusalem, which is a righteous civilization coming down out of heaven from God, linking all human life in an everlasting fellowship of love. Then children shall be no more the accidents of lust, but the offspring of prayer, and every human occupation shall be a communion with God, and the strong shall bear the burdens of the weak, and there shall not be any more pain, and the kingdom of our God shall have come with power.

www.ingramcontent.com/pod-product-compliance
Lightning Source LLC
Chambersburg PA
CBHW020135170426
43199CB00010B/756